Mother. Grave. Ghost.

poems by

Dana Malone and Lauren Suzanne

Finishing Line Press
Georgetown, Kentucky

Mother. Grave. Ghost.

ACKNOWLEDGMENTS

For Lauren Suzanne:
"The Oil Spill" won first place in creative nonfiction category of the Sandra
Hutchins Creative Writing Award in 2018 at Belmont University.

For Dana Malone:
"Ghost hour, a month after my mother's death" was published in *Sinew: 10
Years of Poetry in the Brew*
"The Difference a Death Makes" appeared in a previous manuscript. Thank
you to Lisel Mueller for her editing support years ago.
"Queen of Majesty, the moon and my mother," originally appeared in the
anthology, *All Things Planetary: Poems from featured readers at Flatrock
Open Mic*, 2018.
A different form of "Book review: *An excellent dispute of the accidental*" was
printed as my blurb for *An excellent dispute of the accidental* by Melissa Ford
Thornton, released in 2019.

Publisher: Leah Huete de Maines
Editor: Christen Kincaid
Cover Art: Kristen Chapman
Author Photo (Dana Malone): Kristin Lewis
Author Photo (Lauren Suzanne): Lauren Suzanne
Cover Design: Elizabeth Maines McCleavy

Order online: www.finishinglinepress.com
also available on amazon.com, bookshop.org,
or from your local independent bookseller

Author inquiries and mail orders:
Finishing Line Press
PO Box 1626
Georgetown, Kentucky 40324
USA

Table of Contents

*In memory of my mother and oft-visitor of my dreams,
and Dana's mother as well. —Lauren Suzanne*

*In memory of my mother, singer of lesser-known hymns,
lover of color, and of Janice, Lauren's mother. —Dana Malone*

Introduction by Dana Malone:

Lauren and I are part of a blended family.

—

On March 24, 2017, almost a year after mother died, I attended a reading by Ocean Vuong at Vanderbilt University (the Gertrude and Harold S. Vanderbilt Visiting Writers Series), in support of his poetry collection, *Night Sky with Exit Wounds*. In his presentation, Vuong discussed the nuances of the Vietnamese language. What struck me was his mention that *má, mả,* and *ma* in Vietnamese translate to mother, grave, and ghost, respectively. At that point in time, only a few poems in this collection were in process. The concept of the three meanings of such closely similar words informed the writing and ordering of these poems.

Three summers before it happened

In the backyard of our little house on Harrison Street, a tire swing sits next to a frayed oak, under which the patch of dirt reminds the ground that before the children's feet there was grass.

The yard is not large. It's laced around with a metal gate—and within, a vegetable garden, storage shed, and back porch with four blurry glass chairs, a table, and a grill for steaks and corn on the cob on summer nights when lightning bugs and children roam where they please.

Summer days, porch steps are promises and cicadas are symphonies. As a season, as the whole world keeps moving and we, safe within it.

Spoonfuls of peanut butter and cold sprays of sunscreen protect us from the outside world. My sister digs a burrow to China behind the maple tree and I perform operas for our cats near the lettuce heads.

Here, in the summer on the lawn near the house on the street that memories will not allow to deteriorate. Just like Mom's red hair and Dad's French vanilla coffee creamer, like the always-uncracked concrete, warm to the touch.

Maybe a decade later, there sits a bucket under the water drain filled with algaed water and a vagabond snail or two. Maybe that's after the cancer treatment doesn't work, after the hope for remission has fallen away, after the funeral and after the downcast looks when time moves in the way adults said it always would. Maybe the grass has overgrown the dirt patch, the children have stopped singing to vegetables, the cicadas leave the sky to nest underneath the mournful soil.

The rain cannot touch us here. It cannot hold its weight to the honeysuckle shelter of a child's dream.

Ghost hour, a month after my mother's death

Almost everything can be
forgiven at least

that's what I hoped for.
And shatter-proof
glass from all the things
that could harm me.

Almost everything rests

on her grave
or the touch of my hand
on her shoulder.
What I did not know
would be the last.

Or her palm between
my shoulder blades
all those childhood nights
I did not think
I could dream

that something besides monsters
would be almost everything.

The oil spill/squamous cell cancer

When the oil spilled into the sea, our bedroom walls splashed. The entire house drenched with toxic fluids. Days spent cleaning the walls, months on the floors. At the time, we didn't realize what was gone.

Talking didn't help, even though the counselors didn't pour greasy clichés down our eardrums. The pressure wasn't to talk; it was holding back bright red anger when we heard that old lie, *Everything happens for a reason.* What reason?

Soap washed away the dirt from the playground, but not the everlasting feeling of grimy hair or slick skin. The kids in school stopped noticing our unwashed shirts, ripped jeans. The death look soils the living, too. When our schoolwork came home with oily holes, only the walls of the house pretended not to see.

When the grease-ridden ocean opened up and swallowed her whole, suddenly strangers all knew our story. The second lie: *It gets better.* Third lie: *She'll always be here with you.* But it's we who go home to empty rooms, TV dinners, and salty undulating floors. It's we who are accustomed to the pressure of silence.

Slowly, it all stopped: the car rides home, ice cream for breakfast, sobbing in social studies class.

But still we dug under our fingernails, disbelieved mirrors, asked *Is it in our teeth?* Knowing the oil had seeped into our veins, poisoning the ocean inside us. All fish still swimming were acutely aware of what was missing.

When the oil spilled into the sea, our favorite toys splashed, drowned. Days spent cleaning my room, months on my sister's. In April, we finally asked where our mom, her hospital gown and the IVs and the bloody noses and the pain-ridden smiles and the hand-written bible verses and the stained pillowcases, went.

Years passed and only specks of oil remained. We know filth is ingrained down to subcutaneon. We know some day we'll forgive the well-meaning lies. But sometimes we see the ocean in a rearview mirror or on TV or a friend mentions grease stains and my sister scrubs her hair. I search for hand sanitizer.

The difference a death makes

Mom was 41. I
was 14.

Her nights never let into day. I
treated myself to
maraschino cherries. She
went a while without making
pear halves stuffed with
cottage cheese. Cherries on top.

The curse of losing her mother
and having to live in life-goes-on
haunted her like bedsores
boring, boring, hunting for bone.

Her eyes, a hint
of green and gold, now
hollow underneath
too much sleep. Life crying

                              Bedtime!
around the clock.

Meanwhile, Dad prepared
dinner. Green tomato flesh
hit the skillet.

The evening meal
was cooked with faintest
sizzle

followed by a hush,
the only condiment
during grief.

Your childhood home grows heavier with each new dusting of the earth

Layers of scrap metal form the bars that trace the backyard. Birds nestle in trees. Dogs bark absentmindedly, drifting to sleep in the warmth. *If you jump the fence they'll take you to Azkaban,* my brother says. Our older brother, maker of myths, conjurer of baseball cards, connoisseur of Donkey Kong and Super Smash Bros.

Jenni, the youngest, waves of unkempt hair trailing behind her. She's so unruly. The rest of her can't keep up. There is too much world to see. I, middle child, gatekeeper of silence and sarcasm. I brush my hair one hundred times each night because Nana says *That makes it shiny.*

[...]

There is so much more we could have said but the time spent in the sun, yelling at each other should and must be enough.

Now the gap in space where you should be is its own presence.

Queen of Majesty, the moon and my mother

Depending on the time of month

demure or brightly shining

It is always night
that brings my mother near
as my adolescent arm trembles
it finds her finds the moon
full and right there

Every night
all these years apart
from her earthly form

I make her hair into a French twist
take a lipstick sampler from Avon
I have saved in a dozen moves and purges
give her lips a touch of shade
having perfected the art apart from her.

The makeup case is the same.
Samsonite. Best suited for hats.
Round I go. Lean into form.
The zipper holding to task.

In the full rotation
I remember colors—
melon, pomegranate
cranberry, rose

All the flowers she taught me to name

And now without her, waxing to find the
absences of color the red deep
with so much I do not know of her

Oh holy mystery,
she is the moon and my mother
displays perfect lips and nails
a day after childbirth cannot be
conquered by disease or grief.

My mother with me and the moon the
prick of holly leaf with no white cotton square
to take the blood-drop

The blood irrelevant
in the white as I

wonder what
the moon's arms around me feel like
spinning to another solstice
to that Christmas and every Christmas since

The blank stare, my mother's funeral countenance
my magic father gone with the snow
rushing home from hunt and last-minute shop.

I have always supposed
the moon feels like my mother
smiling, a little pocked and dipped for
missing my father

mostly white like the magnolia bloom
in Savannah Georgia spring

Like the white cotton
of her gown and sheets as I
lay with her

at peak of death

under the open window
the peek-through screen
into night

And we cried

as now I tend to the cry
(of joy mostly
and always in secret)

And say with her
in the silent night
in every crescent
wax, wane

(These These These lives
after deaths This
feeble truth)

Every phase aligned
in the undeniable

every verb ending in

–ing

in my trying to say

Isn't it being a
good-good life.

Her favorite Christmas hymn

There's a song in the air
        Except I always sing
        a *bird*   in the air.

        It's rare to find a bird
        in a candle-lighting service, yes?
        Or squeeze-in-the-pews
        Christmas Eve masses? Oh there's

        Jesus Christ the apple tree. Lots
        of light. Sixteenth note runs
        of *Gloria! Gloria!* The major third
        in Silent Night so difficult by the end of the service,
        wouldn't you say?

        Church night with no nap before it
        The melting wax of you competing with
        how I used to be capable of being
        a soprano with ease. And without you there's

        no rubato of *Honey! Look at those stars!*
        No light guiding as wind's chilling.
        I'm in a hurry to park and run in.
        Deep breath as I release buttoned wool
        slip into a bench warmed by a woman who
        made room for me. Set aside
        the pocketbook you carried
        to my wedding, then I
        to your funeral. I want to say

        Look Mom! It's our pew
        our cozy red velvet.

There's a star in the sky
  Mom, a cardinal's no use sometimes
  and sometimes, it's all I can believe—
  Cardinals flushing white rails,
  spindles of trees.

  Walking pace quarter note equals 120
  to maybe not cry, just rush
  honeycrisps, tangelos, cranberries
  into the house.

  You're absent from any home now else
  I'd show you how sketch pads
  and paper lunch bags are as holy just
  as your double underlines are
  collaborations with greeting cards.

There's a mother's deep prayer
  This nightmare acid's
  ruining your voice.
  All I can do for you is
  in a crown Hallmark
  underline the words I want to say
  gold-sealed and it fits you, Dana.

And a baby's low cry
      1. Choir's nothing quiet as a lullaby
      hiding in your heart in some church pew
      where the repertoire's planned
      scores resting in a folder
      year to year. Once-just-once, could we sing
      the bird song, lesser-known?

      2. Mama, you're hum and Merle Norman.
      Ruby lips and satin.
      Cantata of a woman's circle.
      Velvet everywhere.

      3. If you were with me at the church on West End
      we'd share irreverences:
      I love the candles in plastic
      holders. // Feel his presence. //
      Oh, holy night! // And not burn.

      I'd convince you. Mary's feelings in a king's version—
      inadequate as a winter night and no scarf.
      You not there to see I'm zipped up.

      I'm asking you, mother—
      Send a bird to press red
      into a night without stars.

      4. Cardinal be cradle for
      another Christmas.

A sometime chorus of three siblings, remembered

Watching my mother's heart monitor
A hospital somewhere near Nashville, December 2003

It's almost peaceful how the needle
rises and falls like the beat of a drum
or a basketball on the streaked gym floor.
She lies on the grey hospital bed, so
unassuming, my once mountainous mother.
Three months of tests and IVs,
missed practice, crying sisters who
don't know what loss means. It's not fair.
Becoming a ghost is easy
when your loved ones already write you off as dead.
The Grim Reaper wish from my heart is blasphemous.
I pray for relief, for an end.
I pray for you to flatline.

—Sean, age 13

Why didn't I cry at her funeral?
A child's bedroom in Nashville, February 2004

They said I would get my own room whenever she leaves us
because my big brother would go back to living with his dad. I sat
near the hospital bed, showing Mama stickers from my planner.

One read *bummer* and I told her they misspelled *summer*. She
laughed. Across the room, Nana said, *No baby, it means when*
something sad happens. I smiled and pretended not to understand
that she means right now.

I hate the word *cancer*. It's everywhere on TV commercials. I
wanted them to stop talking about it.

It's just stupid anyway. Daddy said I'm too young to understand but he didn't know I knew Mama was gonna die. It's not a big deal. I'm fine. They said I'm gonna see her when I go to heaven.

When they told us to say bye to mama me and Jenni gave her a quick hug and rushed away. Aunt Kathy told us we were about to go to Chuck E Cheese. I didn't know until the next day she was going away that night. And at the funeral I held a deck of cards, playing war with my friend Anna. Everyone else is crying but I can't. What's wrong with me?

—Lauren, age 8

I miss her
An empty living room, Nashville, March 2004

Da doesn't talk enough. I had to break
something again so he would listen.

I don't know when Mama is
coming home but I can't ask
anymore 'cause Da gets sad.
Lauren tells me to hush. She's
dumb.

I can't go to sleep unless
me and Lauren get to sleep in Da's bed.

I stuck my page of drawings and stickers
next to Mama in her ruffly blue dress
before we went to the cemetery
and said bye. I hope she keeps
it on her 'fridgerator in heaven.

—Jenni, age 6

Cancer

a bristle
>   Sitting with your friend in chemo.
>   No hair or left breast.
>   Brain not up for writing poems.

a crab
>   Lurking on the ocean floor.
>   Snap. There goes your pinky toe. Or so it feels.
>   Your sister, born under Cancer, screams.
>   Wise not to dig.
>   When you want
>   to have fun at Myrtle Beach,
>   you don't care.

the spin of vinyl
>   *Always on my Mind*
>   *Let me be there in your Morning*
>   *Hot Fun in the Summertime*

my mother born July 16
>   Dead two years now. Two.
>   All this lapping of ocean on sand
>   and her footprints still there.
>   North Myrtle. She speed-walked.
>   I could never keep up.

>   Sometimes, the remission reverses
>   some other cause than cancer. That year
>   we made up. She
>   felt proud, and I trusted
>   her joy. I clutched the wheel she
>   trusted my driving.

a memory and mother-reference
    I look to the sky. Needn't go
    beyond the constellation

my mother
    Beta Cancri the brightest
    star in Cancer.
    A foot, really, but I think they call it
    the eye, looking to see
    if I'm eating
    enough. Sober
    enough. Singing
    enough every day.

    Beta Cancri—two hundred light years
    from the sun. A number, she's
    just past my outstretched arms
    pushing towards the sun
    closest when I miss her most.

Cancer as astrological coda

I put on my best mezzo soprano
for her and sing:

Ode to sand.
Ode to ocean.
Ode to sister and mother.
Ode to six stars of
me, slam-dunking.

Ode again to Mom
her potato salad
that garnered more fanfare
than Michael Jordan ever tasted.
To Mom, who thought
Tree Rollins of Clemson was underrated.

Ode to crabs.
Ode to rock-'n'-roll.
To Willie, Olivia and Sly.
Ode to stars.
To seashells and family stones.

Ode to pinch and mercy.
to emerita, unknowing
and everything,
unfinished.

Book review: *An excellent dispute of the accidental*

Fundament to suicide is whimsy.

Working late

What it looks like to be alive in pieces.
Motherless daughter
in fond ephemeral and root.

Piano book. John Thompson Level 3.
Time for intermediate study of Bach.

I love to hear you play while I'm cooking

Your mom takes her life.

Supper's in the fridge

You bake an apple pie with crust edged just so.
Makes her whole again.

I want you to have this, honey

What she never took off.

It opens to time.
Tiny watch inside.
Not your father. Not any man.

Love you, pumpkin!

Blue ink's
life before blood broken. Dried.

The way to distance.

Compass for the ever-present wobble after death.

Subliminal space

(noun) the inhabitation that my mom and nana
take up in the portion of my brain that knows
they are still alive somewhere & I
can hear them, far away.

They only die in my dreams
when daylight is missing
and shadows subsume.
Otherwise, I cannot erase them from my mind,
fully present and breathing and real,
almost close enough to touch.

The dead are only two footsteps away:
one between the earth and the other
between the veil. And it can lift,
you know, but only between two
bottles of wine,
the crevice between night and sunrise,
the distance between your head and the bathwater.

Miles between *I love you* and *Not today,*
a fissure between your high heel point
and the sidewalk, where their salty voices
reach your bone marrow

     —the dead might resurrect themselves

    And that's—
but only long enough to put the car in reverse
       —the gospel truth.

Recitative: (Step)mother squirming in a Midtown church

There is a tenor in the Christmas choir
A doubter with a two-octave range

Crammed on the end of a pew in the back
Hesitant to be in the house of the brutal mystery
The iridescent baby
In exalted shards
Thirty years from slaughter
Lifted high before me
I watch the young man process
Singing *Break forth oh beauteous
heavenly light*

Tight and intricate Bach
Slows the heartbeat
But not the mind

Why he chooses to be some sort of foreigner
In the midst of this place

He is dating a soprano
Maybe that explains it
This spring he will marry her
His mother
(Deceased)
Once of flame and unruly red hair
Will find a way to be there

Every unbelief has a lapse for such a time

The light breaks and blinds
Becomes the dizzy of all we have left undone
The fray of separation
Flares red hot at whatever god
Would rift a bond
Remove a child from his mother

I have figured it out
                              Or think I have
Shaking in her stead

Like her
I am holy enough not to stand him on wood
And desert

Instead

I defend his man bun
Tell everyone
How good he is with sander and nail

Some say his hair is unruly
I wonder
Can he save himself from losing his spot
Under Jesus in the loft
With a rubber band

Unlike the way his mother and I
Couldn't save him
When the tightest tourniquet
Failed on his dehydrated veins
And he screamed
Couldn't take the needle
Barely a thread
For water, electrolyte
Preoperative drug
My lips joining hers in prayers
I didn't know would work

> *Please,*
> *Save our boy*
> *Take the pain in his side*
> *Pierce and let out*
> *The water and gall*
> *Assure us*
> *We got him to the ER in time.*

And so it is,
He lives

Love will say the strangest things
In its fightings and fears yet

Even love that is hoarse
For its drudge
Somehow before snuff of candle
Finds its way to speech.

With Thanks

From Lauren Suzanne:
"Three summers before it happened" and "Your childhood homes grows heavier with each new dusting of the earth" were workshopped in Gary McDowell's Documentary Poetics class at Belmont University in 2019.

I would like to thank the Graduate English Program at Belmont University and my family for supporting me unconditionally.

From Dana Malone:
The lyrics from "There's a song in the air" that title each section of "Her favorite Christmas hymn" were written by poet Josiah A. Holland in 1872. The melody for the version Mom and I sang was by Karl P. Harrington.

These poems were developed in residencies at Sundress Academy for the Arts and through poetry workshops of The Porch Writers Collective. Thank you to facilitators Kate Daniels, Gary McDowell, and Ciona Rouse, along with Bryan Byrdlong, Massey Armistead, Alice Sanford, and other participants. Additional thanks to the critique group of Women Who Write Nashville—Mary Buckner, Judy Klass, Deborah Rankin, Cecelia Tichi and Victoria Webb. Thanks to the Curb Center at Vanderbilt and Vanderbilt-Ingram Cancer Center for supportive space to craft work in this manuscript. Appreciation to Adam Day for reading early drafts of some of these poems and to Pam Evans for first hearing them and for letting me tell her story in "Queen of Majesty."

From both of us:
Special appreciation for the late Michael E. Williams, family member, friend and fellow poet, who published two books with Finishing Line Press and encouraged this effort.

Lauren Suzanne is a writer and poet from Nashville, Tennessee, an alumna of Belmont University, and a graduate of the MAPH program in Art History at the University of Chicago. Her work has appeared in *The Talon Review, The Maine Review, The Crambo*, and the *601*. She won first place in the 2018 Sandra Hutchins Creative Writing Award in Creative Nonfiction at Belmont University. She currently lives in Chicago, Illinois.

Based in Nashville, Tennessee, **Dana Malone** is the recipient of the 2020 poetry prize from Waxing & Waning/Tempest Edition. Her work was accepted for the 2021-2022 *Women Speak* of Women of Appalachia Project, and she recently completed a residency for Art Wire, a collaboration of the Porch Writers Collective and OZ Arts Nashville. Her work has appeared on the podcast, *Versify*; in *Number One, Wordpeace,* and *Native*; on the stages of Tennessee Women's Theater Project; and through #MusicCitySingsAt6.